as above, so below,
as within, so without,
as the universe, so the soul

HERMES TRISMEGISTUS, THE EMERALD TABLET
(2nd - 3rd Century)

Copyright @ 2023 Smudge Tech, Inc
All rights reserved.
ISBN: 9798869791207

SEASONS OF MAGIC

Rituals and Reflections for a Radiant Life

Dedicated to everyone that wishes to live a deeper, more authentic and purposeful life!

Special thanks to the Saged ritual writers and project contributors; Whitney Littlewood, Jennifer Lane, and Marni Sclaroff.

Table of Contents

Welcome . . . 7

Wheel of the Year . . . 9
Moon Phases . . . 10
Moon Calendar . . . 11

Winter . . . 13

Yule . . . 15
Yule Traditions . . . 17
Welcome the Light . . . 18-19
Strengthen Your Boundaries . . . 20
Spellbound . . . 21-22
Dream Into Being . . . 23-24
Yule Blessing . . . 25

Imbolc . . . 27
Imbolc Traditions . . . 29
Blossoming Heart . . . 30-31
Brigid's Blessing . . . 33
Brigid's Cross . . . 34
Grow Your Intentions . . . 35-36
Imbolc Blessing . . . 37

Spring . . . 39

Ostara . . . 41
Ostara Traditions . . . 43
Ostara Rituals:
Tend Your Soul . . . 44-45
Step Over . . . 46
Manifest Abundance . . . 47
Embody Balance . . . 48
Celebrate Earth Day . . . 49-51
Ostara Blessing . . . 52

Beltane . . . 55
Beltane Traditions . . . 56
Jump the Fire . . . 57-58
The Wishing Tree . . . 59

Weaving Yin and Yang . . . 61-62
Sacred Sexuality . . . 63
Self-love Ritual . . . 65-66
Beltane Blessing . . . 67

Summer . . . 69

Litha . . . 71
Litha Traditions . . . 73
Your Solstice Altar . . . 74
Summertime Reflection . . . 75
Solar Greetings . . . 77
Lion's Gate Ritual . . . 78-79
Litha Blessing . . . 80

Lammas . . . 83
Lammas Traditions . . . 84
Spiritual Harvest . . . 85-86
Harvest Reflections . . . 87
Lammas Altar . . . 88
Lammas Blessing . . . 89

Fall . . . 91

Mabon . . . 93
Mabon Traditions . . . 94
Bless This Day . . . 95
Earth Mandala . . . 97
Equinox Water Ritual . . 99
Reciprocity Reflections . . . 100
Mabon Blessing . . . 101

Samhain . . . 103
Samhain Traditions . . . 105:
Beloved Ancestors . . . 106
The Dumb Supper . . . 107
RIP Ritual . . . 109
Know Thy Shadow . . . 110-114
Book of Shadows . . . 115

Samhain Blessings . . . 116

Welcome

In a world that often rushes by, we find ourselves yearning for a deeper connection to ourselves, the people around us and nature itself. We crave meaning, purpose, and a sense of wonder that transcends the ordinary and brings us face to face with the extraordinary. These experiences are within everyone's reach and the wonders of life on earth are accessible, free and available to all. You just have to slow down, look closely, tap into your imagination, and believe!

Our ancestors, from cultures all over the world, have left us with wisdom, guidance and rituals through which we can achieve higher states of consciousness. States that connect us deeply to the world around us, letting us grow and flow in nature's rhythm. We can tap into these divine states for guidance, support, healing and empowerment simply by tuning into our breath, clarifying our intentions and backing it all up with right action. The life you love to live is within reach, and "Seasons of Magic" is here to support you on your soul's journey.

"Seasons of Magic" is full of rituals, traditions, inspiration and reflections designed to align you with the rhythm of the seasons and the rhythm of your soul. We are guided by our Sun as we travel through the seasons of life, not just in the meteorological sense, but in the cycles of our personal growth and transformation. As we navigate the ever-turning wheel of time, we are presented with opportunities for renewal and revelation as the earth around us guides the way.

And while the Sun sets the stage for the grand seasons of life on Earth, the Moon guides the smaller cycles. The fluctuation of rising and falling tides, the revealing and concealing of our souls, and the accumulation and release of energy, ideas, people and experiences all wax and wane with the Moon above.

Together, over this next year, we will synch with nature through rituals for deeper self-discovery and transformation. These rituals are the key to unlocking the hidden potential that lies within you. You'll gain the power to manifest your dreams, release what no longer serves you, and weave a life that is deeply authentic and rich with purpose.

Each ritual is offered here only as a guide. Our most powerful soul magic comes from each of our unique experiences, intentions, and needs. Use these rituals as outlines, ideas and energetic imprints but make each of them your own. There are no rules!

As you embark on this journey, know that you are not alone. You are joined by countless seekers who, like you, are yearning for a life of greater meaning and authenticity. The seasons are your guides, and the rituals are your tools, together illuminating the path towards a life filled with a profound connection to your Highest Self and the world around you.

So, with an open heart and a curious spirit, let us embark on this enchanting journey together. Travel with us through the Celtic Year of the Wheel practicing rituals to ride the seasons of magic. Spin the wheel to dream, manifest, divine, heal, surrender and ignite your soul - the time is now!

In gratitude,
Julia
Founder of Saged

Wheel of the Year

The Celtic Wheel of the Year is a set of eight Sabbats, or holy days, based on earlier Pagan celebrations of the Sun's journey across the skies. The four Grand Sabbats, or Cross-Quarter Days, are Imbolc, Beltane, Lammas and Samhain. The Grand Sabbats celebrate the peak energy of each season. There are also four Lesser Sabbats, what we think of as the balancing and tipping points of the equinoxes and solstices, known as Yule, Ostara, Litha and Mabon.

Each holiday has its own unique traditions, rituals and celebrations that honor the energy of the seasons of winter, spring, summer and fall as well as the rising and falling tides that flow one into another. Each season also holds an elemental energy - earth in the winter, air in the spring, fire in the summer and water in the fall. We flow through the year as we flow through life, being born, growing, maturing, dying and releasing into the unknown, to dream back into being for the next cycle.

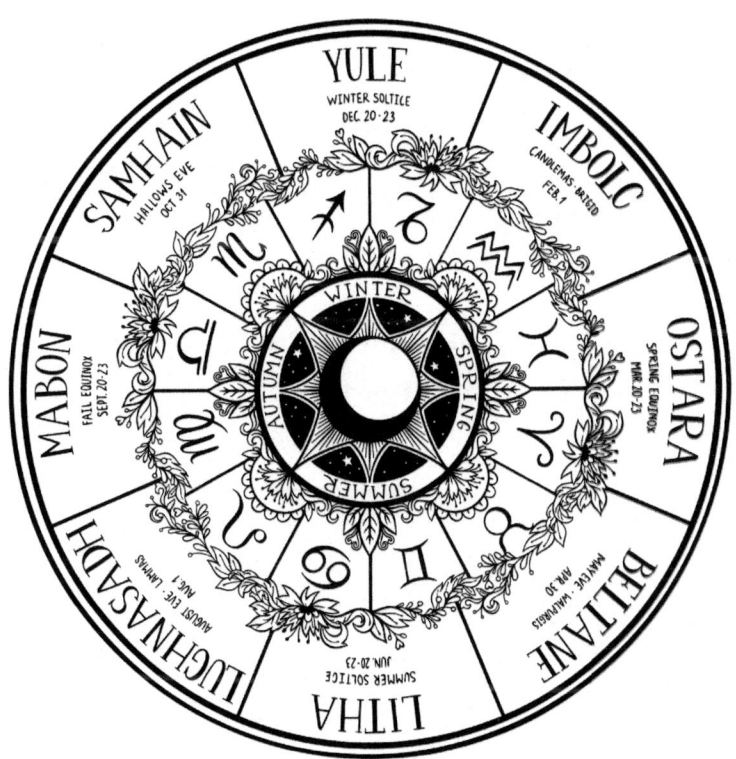

Moon Phases

New or Dark Moon - The beginning of the cycle - set your intentions.

Waxing Crescent - The sliver is growing! Focus on supporting your intention by making a plan.

First Quarter - Half the moon is visible, it's time to take action.

Waxing Gibbous - The moon is getting fuller each day and the energy is rising. Hold on for the ride!

Full Moon - The moon is full in the sky and it's time to celebrate the culmination of the cycle! After the peak it's time to release.

Waning Gibbous - The moon slumps heavy in the sky, continue releasing what no longer serves.

Last Quarter - The opposite half of the moon is visible. We are completing our transformation.

Waning Crescent or Balsamic Moon - Only a sliver is left in the cycle, reflect and integrate the lessons of the past cycle.

MOON CALENDAR

2024

January

03   11   17   25

February

02   09   16   24

March

03   10   17   25

April

01   08   15   23

May

01   07   15   23   30

June

06   14   21   28

July

05   13   21   27

August
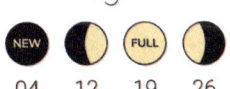
04   12   19   26

September

02   11   17   24

October
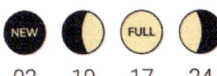
02   10   17   24

November

01   09   15   22

December

01   08   15   22   30

Winter

Winter

The quarter of the year from Samhain to Imbolc, from fall to winter, in the Northern Hemisphere, is when the days get shorter, the nights longer and the temperatures begin to drop. As the vibrant tapestry of autumn's colors fade, and the whisper of a chill touches the air, we find ourselves at the threshold of a profound transformation. The change in energy from fall to winter is a time of the falling tide, a time of releasing and surrendering to the unknown.

The shift from fall to winter is also a time to embrace the shadows, to honor the wisdom of the crone, and to delve into the mysteries of the dark half of the year. It is a time of stillness, a time of contemplation, a time to dream and a time to quietly accept the truth of our lives.

Just as nature retreats within for rest and rejuvenation, as the trees drop their leaves and pull nutrients back down to their roots, we pull our energy and awareness inward and down into the core of our being. As the Sun seems temporarily overtaken by darkness, life on earth slows down and our inner world opens up for reflection and quiet contemplation. At this threshold we reflect on the past and begin to dream of the future, staying rooted to the present through firelight, family and the comforts of home.

This is the season to integrate the events and changes you have gone through in the last year. How have both your inner and outer worlds changed? How have you grown? What have you lost and what have you gained? What lessons of life will you hold onto as you move into the next cycle of the year?

Open your heart, mind and deep imagination and let the seeds of beginning take root in your being. This year can be your most magical year yet if you focus, trust and believe. There is a power within you that is germinating, growing and preparing to be seen, shared and appreciated.

But for now, rest deeply. Review the past, dream of the future while being completely present to this moment, this breath, this day. Honor where you have been and the people that have come before you and surrender to the deep wisdom and abundance of earth's magic. All is coming!

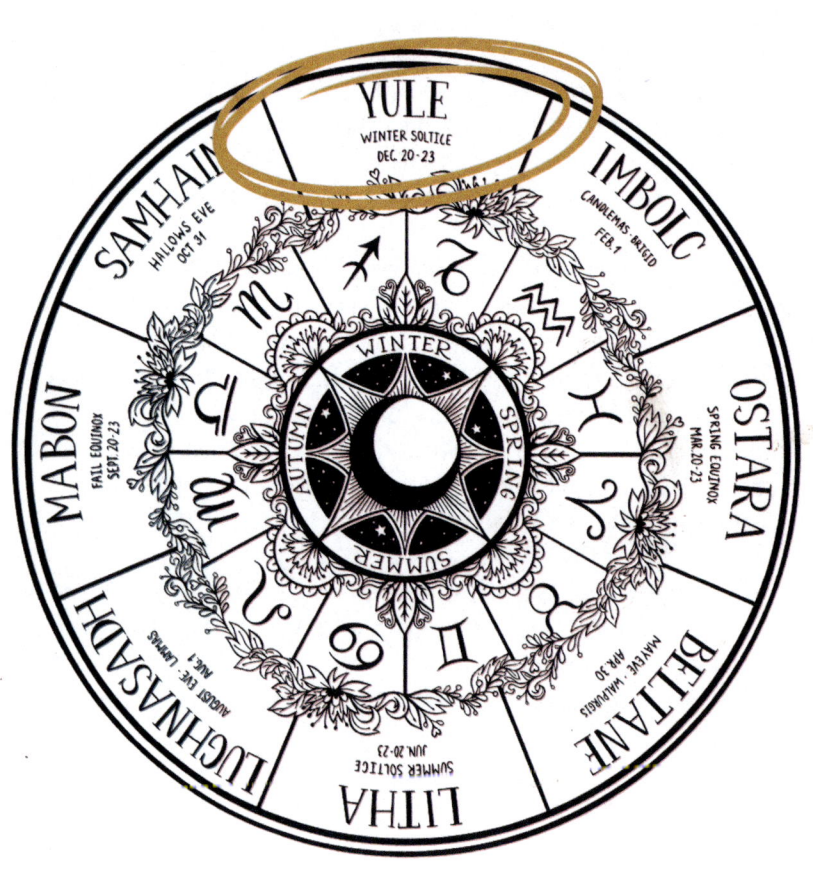

YULE
Winter Solstice
(December 21 - 23)

Yule marks the longest night of the year in the Northern Hemisphere and the shortest night in the Southern Hemisphere. Yule occurs between the 21st and 23rd of December each year when the tilt of the Earth's axis is farthest from the sun. Astrologically, this is the day the Sun moves into the earth sign of Capricorn in the tropical zodiac system.

Yule celebrates the return of the sun, the victory of light over dark and the relief and gratitude that comes as the days grow longer and warmer. Life goes on and we are here to experience another season!

Yule is the point in the Earth's dance around the Sun when it reaches the furthest point in its orbit before swinging back again, like a pendulum, to the height of summer. Imagine the relief of our ancestors when the Sun temporarily stands still in the sky before turning back in the other direction. This was a time of great celebration. They made it to the height of winter and now there is again hope for warm days, healthy crops and hunting - life as they have known it, continues.

However, at Yule there is still a long, cold and dark winter ahead. The energy is one of renewal but also fortitude. Gratitude and hope mingle together as families gather around the fire calling in abundance for the year to come.

Dreams and visions of the future dance like sugarplum fairies in our heads. This is a time of great transition - a time of death and rebirth, a sacred pause between cycles. This is the time to fertilize the ground of possibility for the life you will live over the comi burns brig

Come to the hearth and get comfortable, have a warm drink and bring your favorite blanket. It's time to turn your awareness inward and tend the inner flame of your spirit.

Remember, without the darkness, there is no light!

Whose woods these are I think I know.
His house is in the village, though;
He will not see me stopping here
To watch his woods fill up with snow.

My little horse must think it queer
To stop without a farmhouse near
Between the woods and frozen lake
The darkest evening of the year.

He gives his harness bells a shake
To ask if there's some mistake.
The only other sound's the sweep
Of easy wind and downy flake.

The woods are lovely, dark, and deep,
But I have promises to keep,
And miles to go before I sleep,
And miles to go before I sleep.

ROBERT FROST

Yule Traditions

Yule marks the longest night of the year as well as the tipping point and return of the sun. Hope is alive at Yule but there is still a long winter to get through. These Yule traditions celebrate both the light and the dark.

Fire: Fire is the ultimate representation of the energy of the sun. Celebrate Yule with a fire in your hearth, a bonfire outside or lighting black and white candles in your home.

Yule Altar: Although nature may be sleeping, there is still beauty all around. Collect the natural gifts of the season to decorate your altar like pinecones, holly, berries, nuts and dried fruit.

The Yule Log: Make your hearth fire or bonfire extra special by adding a Yule log. Adorn your log with decorations, douse it with cider or ale and stay around it until it fully burns. While it burns let go of the last year and add energy to your intentions for the next cycle of the sun.

Smudge Your Space: Cleanse your space with the scents of the season! Make a smudge bundle out of dried pine, fir, rosemary or juniper. Welcome the energy of renewal and potential into your home.

Mistletoe: Hang mistletoe above your threshold and doorways to welcome love and positivity into your home through the rest of winter.

Yule Ritual:
Welcome the Light

Clear your calendar the evening of Yule and plan a place that you can go that is quiet and peaceful and you have a view of the setting sun. You don't necessarily need to travel to a special location, you can just go outside or to a window as the sun begins to set. Once you find your special place, take time to settle your energy. This is a night to feel into positive disintegration and release. Notice the light, breathe in the air and connect to the ground of being. If you like, imagine yourself like a snow globe with all of your energy gently falling and settling around you.

While the light fades say goodbye to the last year. Give thanks for all of your experiences - for the joy they may have brought as well as the opportunities for growth. Travel through the year remembering the ups and downs, the achievements, the surprises, the celebrations and tribulations. Remember any of the people or animals that might have been lost. If you feel open, use this time to discuss the past year with friends and family. You can find a special object, like a pinecone, to pass around as each person shares about their past year. Open your ears and your hearts to each person present and show them your support as the light slowly fades.

Stay in this gentle meditative space until the sun is down and it is completely dark. With the last ray of light say goodbye to the past and anything else that feels right in the moment.

Then, either stay outside and light a fire (please follow proper safety precautions). Or, go inside and light your fireplace, Yule log or candles. Feel free to get creative with your Yule candles - you can decorate them, curve symbols into them and coordinate their colors with your intentions. If you are with friends, be sure to have a candle for each of you.

Now, gaze into the fire and pull your energy into the center of your being. Feel your spirit at the center of your being grow in warmth and light. Think about what you are birthing into your life for this next year. Try to come up with just a few simple goals, to help you focus. If you'd like, take turns sharing intentions with your family and friends.

Let the light of the flame, and the energy of the returning sun, kindle hope deep in your soul for the year to come.

Yule Intentions

What are you birthing into your life this next cycle of the Sun?

1. ....

2. ....

3. ....

4. ....

5. ....

Strengthen Your Boundaries

On the night of Yule, the Sun moves into the strong, determined, and grounded sign of Capricorn. Capricorn season offers us the opportunity to clarify our boundaries. It is especially a good time to remember that all healthy relationships thrive in a balance of openness, vulnerability and clearly expressed needs and wants.

Boundaries are the things that we say "NO" to. They are the things that are not ok with us.

Your intuition will show you where your boundaries are through the emotions of anger, resentment, and irritability. You know that a boundary has been crossed when you feel any of the anger type emotions, and then it is important for you to find a way to express and clarify it.

Boundaries are sexy! Clarifying your boundaries and letting other's know exactly what you are ok with and what you are not reflects your confidence, self-love and self-respect. Clear boundaries honor the inherent dignity of all beings, and what could be sexier then that?

If you feel anger, resentment, or agitation in an area of your life, notice what boundary has been crossed, and decide what you need to do to clarify it. Sometimes simply communicating your feelings to anther can improve the situation. Other times you might be ready for bigger changes. Let the strong, determined confidence of Capricorn support you – it's time to stand in your full power!

Spellbound

We exist in a great matrix of energy, and everything is connected. We know that there is more than the visible world, and that there are multiple dimensions to reality.

Energy is real, and words are built of energy vibrations. They begin as a thought vibration, and then we move them through the body to send this energy out into the world.

This is why we call magical spells, SPELLS. We are shaping reality by "spelling", or directing our words in very specific ways.

Thoughts become words and words become actions and actions become your reality. Respect the power of the words you use. They ripple out and leave an energetic imprint on the energy field around you.

What energy are you calling into your life? What spell are you casting on the world around you? Remember - do as you like as long as you harm none!

Dream your dreams and cast your spell! The Universe is listening, and waiting to help you!

> By the moon and stars,
> my desires take flight,
> In the coming year,
> bathed in magical light.
> As I will, so mote it be,
> Blessings and magic,
> in the year to be!

Spellbound

Write your spell here. Make it short and sweet - extra special power granted when it rhymes!

So mote it be!

Dream into Being

The invitation of winter is to slow down, go within and dream!

As you hibernate this winter in your warm and cozy bed, listen deeply to the mythic and metaphorical world of your dreams. Your dreams are the messengers of your soul and when we dream deeply the symbols breakthrough from the subconscious to the conscious mind, often in divine timing, to guide our lives.

Our dreamworld connects us to our deep imagination and although sometimes cryptic, our dreams carry a truth and weight that can shake us awake to parts of our lives and ourselves that we have blocked or forgotten.

Before you go to bed, call in your desire for meaningful dream messages! Start by connecting with your spirit guides. Say their names out loud (Gods, Goddesses, Ancestors, Angels, Elementals, etc.) and ask them to come to you and give you the guidance you need to live your highest truth. Thank them for their wisdom and support. Then, go to sleep! You can aid your dreaming by putting crystals under your pillow.

If you wake from a dream, write it down immediately. It helps to have a special dream journal by your bed. Remember the small details, the people and the feelings. When interpreting your dream make sure to look at it symbolically, not literally. The people in your dreams often represent other people in your life. Approach the meaning like a mysterious riddle meant only for you!

May you be open to guidance from the other realms and its infinite wisdom!

Dream Journal

Yule Blessing

At Yule's embrace, as shadows fall,
We heed the ancient, mystic call.
In the darkest night, we stand tall,
To manifest dreams, we give our all.

With candles aglow and intentions clear,
We harness the magic of this time of year.
From our hearts, we release all fear,
As dreams take root and draw near.

With the solstice's return, and the sun's warm ray,
May your dreams shine brighter, day by day.

So mote it be, as the wheel does spin,
May your dreams take flight, and new life begin.

IMBOLC
The Stirring of Spring
(February 2)

On the 2nd of February, when the Sun is exact at 15 degrees of Aquarius, we celebrate the Grand Sabbat, or Cross-Quarter holiday of Imbolc! Imbolc is the Celtic Holy Day that honors the very first breaths of spring. Imbolc means "in the belly", or "in the womb" referring to the time of year when all of life is gestating in the womb of the earth. The miracle of life is working its magic beneath the layers of ice and soil, preparing itself for the next cycle!

At Imbolc, the world may still be draped in the chill of winter, but beneath the snow and frost, the earth is awakening. It's a time when the first delicate crocuses and snow drops push through the thawing soil and the days noticeably lengthen. The energy of Imbolc is a whisper of the promise of rebirth, the spark of renewal after the deep slumber of winter.

Imbolc is associated with the Celtic goddess Brigid, the patroness of poetry, healing, smithcraft and keeper of the hearth. Her presence infuses the season with creativity and inspiration. Brigid embodies poetry, protection, healing and blessings. Goddess Brigid became St. Brigit during the Christianization of Europe and she is still revered today in many parts of Ireland and the UK.

Although the stirrings of spring can be felt at Imbolc, this is still a time of cold and darkness. It was only recently in the evolution of humans that we have electric lights and heat in our houses. Our ancestors had a lot of time in the winter spent inside by the fire. This is when the simple arts of poetry, singing, music and stories were shared. This was a time of year for gathering together, laughing and getting through the cold times together, with the blessings of Brigid, protector of the sacred flame.

The energy of Imbolc is a gentle yet persistent force, urging us to cast off the shadows of the past and embrace the potential of the future. It's a time to kindle the fires of our intentions, nurturing them as they grow and unfurl like the first green shoots of spring. Imbolc reminds us that even in the darkest of times, a spark of light and life remains, ready to flourish once more.

"There is always in February, some one day, at least, when one smells the yet distant but surely coming, summer."

GERTRUDE JEKYLL

Imbolc Traditions

Imbolc marks the midpoint between the winter solstice and the spring equinox. It's a time of purification, initiation, and manifestation. Many Imbolc traditions honor the coming season of light and the fertility of the earth it will bring.

Candle Lighting: Light candles, particularly white or yellow ones, to welcome back the sun.

Brigid's Crosses: Create a Brigid's crosses from reeds or straw to invoke the protection and blessings of the Celtic goddess Brigid. Hang your cross over your threshold or in your windows to share with your neighbors.

Imbolc Altar: Imbolc is associated with the lactation of ewes and the first signs of new life. Make offerings of milk, cheese, and butter to Brigid and the spirits of your land to ensure a bountiful year.

Smudge Your Space: Cleanse your space with sacred herbs to wash away any lingering negative energy. Or, start your early spring cleaning!

Visit Sacred Springs and Wells: Seek out and spend time near sacred springs or wells. Leave offerings of gratitude.

Divine: Practice divination for guidance related to the coming year. Ask about big decisions you need to make. Try working with a pendulum or reading your own Tarot cards. Tap into the unseen for wisdom and support.

Imbolc Ritual:
Blossoming Heart

This is a ritual to help you embody the blossoming of your heart and your life, like the blossom of a flower in springtime. As you practice this ritual, feel into the energy of becoming, of growing, of blooming and of maturing into your fullest, truest self. Feel how these urges are inherent in the entire Universe – sun, moon, earth and stars are all in various stages of becoming. Align with the essence of universal life force above, below and within you.

Start by creating sacred space. Sprinkle salt and water around you in a circle, light a candle and smudge your space with some sacred smoke or incense. In doing this, you are invoking the elements of earth, water, fire and air.

Now, lie down, sit or settle into child's pose in the center of your circle. Whatever shape you choose, feel yourself close to the Earth and breathe into this holy relationship.

Then, clasp your hands tightly together and SQUEEZE! As you do so, feel into these words from Anais Nin:

"Life is truly known only to those who suffer loss, endure adversity and stumble from defeat to defeat."

Contemplate how life has shaped and pressed you to grow. Remember that the brilliance of the diamond is only formed under immense pressure. Then gently, slowly release your hands, imagining your energy softening and opening to life's renewal.

Feel into these words from Anais Nin:

"And the day came when the risk to remain tight in a bud was more painful than the risk it took to blossom."

Know that you are always in a process of becoming,. Let the rich quiet of winter rejuvenate and soothe your soul so you can bloom in your full glory this spring!

Imbolc Reflection

What is blossoming in you that can no longer be denied?

"I will lead you home,
I will guide you back,
My waters will carry thee,
My flame will guide thee."

"SEA SONG FROM BRID"
GEMMA MCGOWAN

Brigid's Blessing

Blessed season of inspiration and anticipation!

For this ritual you will need a flower. Your flower can be store bought or found. It can be real or symbolic. If you don't have a flower to use find a picture, drawing or carving. Goddess Brigid loves your creativity and handiwork!

Once you've found your flower, gently cup it in your hands. Connect with the light around you from 360 degrees, especially the light cradled underneath you in the womb of Gaia.

Soften your eyes and gaze at the flower. Really see it in detail and nuance. Open to the teachings of this flower - the life cycle, the tenderness, the resiliency, the promise, the purpose, the beauty. Breathe deeply and honor all the ways you are also blossoming, both the vulnerability and strength required to show up for yourself and others, season after season.

Bring the flower in your cupped hands to your lips and gently speak into the flower your prayers, thoughts, hopes and intentions for yourself, the ones you love and the whole world. Blow your breath into the center of the flower to inprint it with your unique Spirit!

Now, make this flower an offering. You can place it on your altar (if it's something you made), or you can offer it to the earth outside in a special place.

When you see this flower remember how you to are still growing, blooming and becoming your full self! May the light and warmth of Brigid's blessings be yours - here, now and always.

Brigid's Cross

Brigid (pronounced "Breede" with a soft rolling "r") is the Goddess of Imbolc. She blesses us with inspiration, protection and healing. The symbol of Brigid's cross is a way to connect with this energy.

Materials Needed:
1. **Reeds or Straw:**
   - Choose long, pliable reeds or straw. Traditionally rushes were used.
2. **Scissors or Pruners**

Instructions:
1. Collect a handful of reeds. The number you'll need depends on the size you want your cross to be, but a good starting point is around 20-30 reeds.
2. Trim the reeds to a uniform length, typically 9-12 inches. If the reeds are too long, they become difficult to work with.
3. To make the reeds more pliable, you can soak them in water for a few hours.
4. Take two reeds and overlap them to form a "plus" sign (cross). The center where they overlap is the center of your cross.
5. Layer additional reeds on top of the base, one at a time. Place each new reed over the previous one, alternating between horizontal and vertical positions.
6. As you add more reeds, weave them over and under the existing ones. Continue until you've reached the desired size for your cross.
7. Once you've woven the arms to your satisfaction, secure the ends by tucking them under other reeds or tying them together. Trim the ends to create an even appearance.
8. Let it dry fully before hanging it up to display!

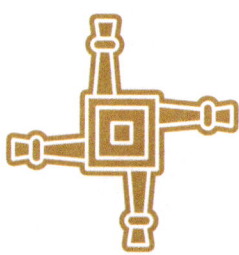

Grow Your Intentions

Imbolc is a time when the nebulous dreams and visions of the dark winter months start to come into focus as the days lengthen and signs of life emerge from the frosty ground.

This is a time to start planting seeds of intention. What you give attention to grows and comes into being. Whether its science or magic, who knows! But one thing is clear, your dreams in life are worth your attention!

Start by collecting some seeds that you will grow indoors and then transfer outside when they are big and strong enough. Leeks, onions, tomatoes, peppers and cucumbers are all good choices! Get your starter soil, find a sunny south-facing window (and/or extra florescent lighting) and set out your supplies where you have space. Label your starter pots and put earth in each one.

Then, ground yourself and take a few deep breaths. Bring your hands over the soil and offer gratitude to the earth and the magical power of the soil to grow food! Choose a seed and hold it in your hand, make an association between the plant you are growing and an intention for your life that is alive in your heart at this moment.

For example, you might say "as this tomato grows plump and juicy so will my love life!" or "as this leek grows tall and confident I will stand in my full power!" Get creative and make it meaningful to you. You can even write the words "love" and "power" on your pots for extra energy.

Then, plant the seed in the soil while you visualize your intention. Take the time to think about how it feels and what it means to have a plump and juicy love life! Or, what it really means to stand in your power. Infuse the seed and it's life with your intention! Then, bless your seed with water, blow on it to give it your energy, pat the soil and put it in the sun! All elemental energies accounted for, you are ready to sit back and watch your "veg-tentions" grow!

And as they grow so will your dreams and visions. Happy planting!

Plant Your Intention

Label this pot or draw your "veg-tentions" here!

Imbolc Blessing

In the deep dark of winter,
may you find your inner light.

In the dark night of the soul,
may you be held by the moon and stars,
with hope in your heart for a new day.

May you cherish the warmth and comfort of your home.
May you cherish the laughter and love of family and friends.
May you cherish the abundance of the earth.

All is here for you.
You are here for all.
Dream your biggest dream,
answer your biggest call.

And so it is. And so it shall be!

Spring

SPRING

The quarter of the year from Imbolc to Beltane, from mid-February through mid-May in the Northern Hemisphere, is the time of lengthening days, warmer weather and the blooming of new life. It is when all is fresh and new and possible! The rising tide of solar energy from winter to spring has a profound effect on all of us as we shed the cloak of winter and embrace the lightness of spring, a time of exuberance and inspiration. Like the sprouting buds that peek through the soil, we too emerge into the world with a childlike wonder, shaking off the remnants of stagnation.

As one season gives way to another in the physical world, the same cyclical pattern happens in our lives. We don't ever finally emerge and stay in the light of happiness; we also don't stay in the darkest night forever. There is always the coming and going, the highs and lows, the light and dark.

This journey from darkness to light is a rebirth, a chance to reinvent ourselves and breathe new life into our dreams. We dance, sing, and celebrate the wonders of nature, for it is a gift to be granted another chance to live fully and joyfully. As winter dreams give way to spring blossoms, remember that everything you desire, you deserve!

As we welcome spring, life on earth awakens and the pulse of nature quickens. We emerge from our homes, ready to get outside and enjoy the abundance of nature all around us. Spring is a time of sexuality, fertility and celebration. Weave this radiant air energy into your spells. Plant your intentions in the fertile soil and let your creativity bloom! Tap into your unique gift for the world and nurture it this spring. The earth and all beings everywhere need your magic!

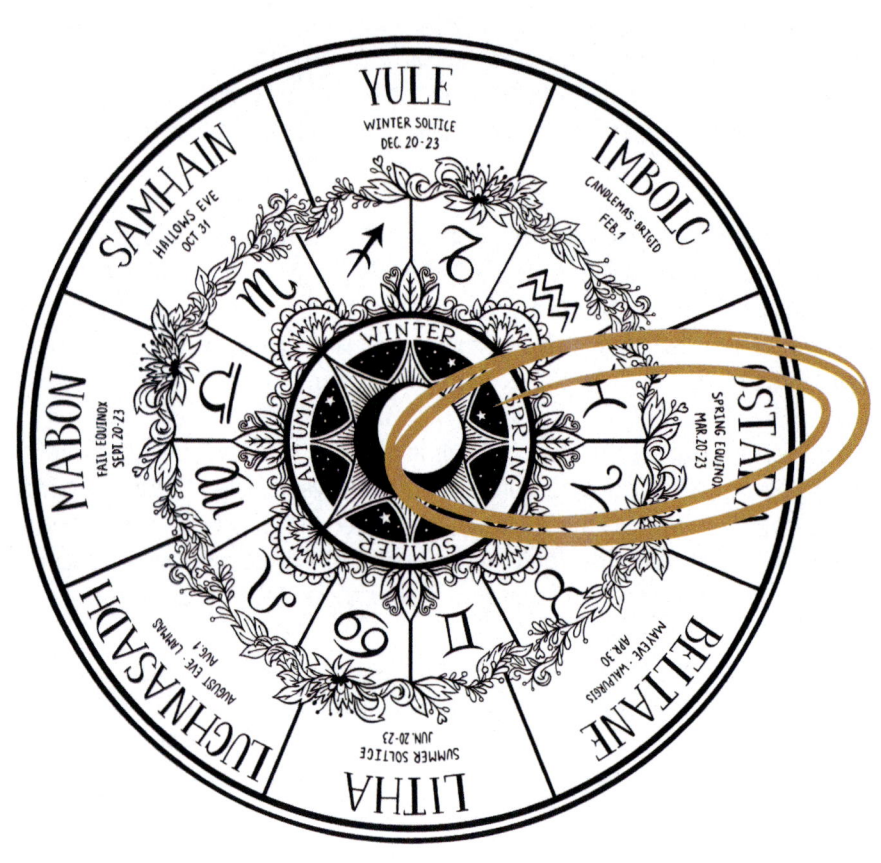

OSTARA
Vernal Equinox
(March 20 - 21st)

Ostara is celebrated around the vernal equinox (usually March 20th-21st) and marks the potent moment in the Wheel of the Year when the balance of light and dark is equal. After this sacred pause, the Earth tips toward the full bloom of spring. This celebration resonates with the energy of renewal, balance, and the awakening of life.

Astrologically, Ostara aligns with the sun's entrance into the zodiac sign of Aries. Aries, the first sign of the zodiac, is characterized by its fiery, pioneering spirit. As the sun moves into Aries, it brings a burst of dynamic energy and initiative. This alignment signifies the spark of new life and the surge of vitality that characterizes this season. It's a time to embrace new beginnings, set intentions, and harness the bold, initiatory energy of Aries to manifest your desires.

Ostara represents balance and harmony. Day and night are of equal length, symbolizing the equilibrium between light and dark forces. It's a moment to reflect on the balance we seek in our lives and the harmony we aim to achieve. This balance extends to our connection with the Earth and the honoring of the cycles of nature.

Ostara is also a season of fertility, symbolized by the eggs and hares associated with the holiday. Align with nature's rhythms and tap into the dynamic forces of renewal, balance, and growth this Ostara by celebrating the Earth's awakening and nurturing your aspirations!

"A little Madness in the Spring
Is wholesome even for the King."

EMILY DICKINSON

Ostara Traditions

Ostara is a time of hope and renewal, and these traditions reflect the themes of fertility, growth, and celebration that come with the arrival of spring.

Egg Decorating: Color and decorate eggs to symbolize all that you are birthing at this time in your life! Red eggs are particularly powerful symbols of rising energy and life force!

Spring Cleaning: Out with the old, in with the new! This is a time to cleanse and declutter your home.

Plant Seeds: Start your garden on Ostara! You can plant your intentions with your vegetables.

Celebrate Sunrise: Gather at sunrise to welcome the increasing daylight and offer gratitude to the Sun.

Honey: Gather, buy or gift honey to friends and family as a symbol of spring's sweet abundance.

Eostre's Hare: Decorate your home or community with the symbol of the hare. The hare is associated with Eostre, the Germanic Goddess that Ostara is named after and represents fertility and magic.

Balance Rituals: Bring equilibrium into all aspects of your life by balancing your chakras. You can do this through breathwork, chanting and visualization.

Ostara Ritual:
Tend Your Soul

In Spring, our energetic roots reach down deep into the center of the earth where we connect with the beating heart, the Anima Mundi or soul of the world! All is buzzing with life, with wonder and with excitement!

Ride this wave of energy to tend to your inner garden. We are all products of nature and nuture. This spring bring extra care to your environment. Internally and externally, are you in a place where you can thrive and your dreams can flourish?

What are you nurturing, nourishing and tending to in your life? What seeds of intention did you plant at Imbolc? What dreams are ready to spring to life? Are there parts of your being that are calling for more light, more energy, more nutrients or more joy?

 Imagine your life as a garden. Are your roots strong enough? Are your budding flowers getting enough sunlight? Are you getting enough water or maybe too much? Is the ecosystem of your being working in symbiotic harmony? Or, is there a certain shade, lack or weed that needs to be dealt with?

Tune in to how you can nourish your inner garden so it flourishes. With the analogy of the garden in mind, take stock of what you need to survive (love, touch, connection, safety, etc.) and what you need to thrive (energy, passion, strength, joy, etc.) Are there small steps you can take today towards creating the life conditions in which you and your dreams can thrive?

Ostara Reflection

How are you tending your soul garden? Are you surviving or thriving?

Step Over

As we experience the spring equinox, we are ushered over a threshold. Thresholds are sacred moments (and places) where the soul's journey can be revealed with more clarity and connection. Practice this ritual on or as close to the equinox as possible. This is a time to reflect on the past, enjoy a sacred pause in the present moment, and invite in the future.

Try this ritual to embody the equinox and traverse this threshold with gratitude, intention and hope!

Start by drawing a line on the ground - you can do this outside with chalk, or place a string/stick on the ground. Then, stand on one side of the line, reflecting on the past 6 months of the year. What have you accomplished? What have you learned?

When you are ready, take a single step and stand with one foot on either side of the line. While straddling the line, become aware of the present moment by focusing on your breath. Consciously inhale for 4 counts, hold the breath for 4 counts, and then exhale for 4 counts and hold your breath out for 4 counts. Through the breath, bring all of yourself to this threshold moment.

Then, step over to the other side, and as you do, invite the light of grace and love to be with you as you step into the future! Keep your dreams alive in your heart as you open to the gifts of the Universe!

Manifest Abundance

As you inhale, silently say the words:

"I lovingly receive the gifts of life."

As you exhale, silently say the words:

"I lovingly give the gifts of life."

Let the energy flow. Feel your inner body expand, feel your inner light glow.

As you expand your capacity for giving and receiving energy, abundance will be able to flow to you and from you in bigger, more impactful ways.

Embody Balance

The equinoxes, sacred moments of balance between light and dark, remind us to nurture all parts of ourselves. To let ourselves be free and grounded, to be happy and sad, to give and to receive.

Take a few moments today to come home to your body and your breath by embodying balance through practicing tree pose or 'vrkasana'.

~ Stand up tall with your shoulders back, feet hip distance apart, and toes spread.
~ Shift your weight over to your left leg and slide the inside of your right foot to your left inner thigh (or calf or ankle).
~ Press your standing foot into the Earth, feel it growing deep and strong roots. Press your raised foot into your leg and fire up the energy of your midline.

~ Lift both arms up overhead and into a wide "V".
~ Take 5 deep breaths, inhaling energy from the earth up your body and exhaling it back to the earth. Then, repeat on the other side.

Try doing this outside amongst the trees. They love it when we imitate them in all their glory.

May you be strong, clear, balanced and in alignment today and everyday!

Celebrate Earth Day

"You cannot get through a single day without having an impact on the world around you."
- Jane Goodall

We are living in a time of great upheaval on our planet. We are experiencing the effects of our human behaviors on the Earth including habitat loss, climate change, species extinction, and pollution in our air, water and soil. But, this is also a time of awakening. Many people are starting to understand that everything is an interwoven, interconnected web and are taking responsibility for their own behavior. We know that whatever we do to the Earth, we also do to ourselves.

What will you do today to help mend our planet? Will you offer a blessing or gratitude? Plant a tree? Leave an offering for the spirits of the land where you live? Create an outdoor shrine? Tend to your garden? Donate to an organization doing good work in the world?

There are many ways to contribute to what environmental activist and Buddhist scholar Joanna Macy calls "The Great Turning." This is the moment in time when we value the life force inherent in the Earth itself and move beyond the idea that all of life exists to meet the needs of humans. It doesn't have to be about money or your time. The crisis we find ourselves in is a spiritual one as much as it is material and therefore we can begin the healing through our reverence, our appreciation and our wonder at the world around us.

Try this today:

Stand outside with bare feet. Close your eyes, and feel the ground beneath your feet, the air touching your skin, and the sun on your face. As you breathe, know that you are breathing with the trees, the birds, the animals and the gently pulsation of the Earth. Feel the exchange of energy and support and send prayers to the earth, the air, the water, the fire, the sun, the moon, the stars and the more-than-human spirits all around you! Press your feet into the ground as you lift your arms to the sky, feel your spirit rise as you lower your arms. Do this movement a few times until you feel your energy lit up and creating a channel, a living conduit, between earth and sky. All is living, all is sacred. And so it is.

"The care of the Earth is our most
ancient and most worthy,
and after all,
our most pleasing responsibility.

To cherish what remains of it,
and to foster its renewal,
is our only legitimate hope."

WENDELL BERRY

Earthly Love

Write a love poem, spell or love note for our planet.

Ostara Blessing

Gentle forces of the cosmos,
I call upon you this sacred eve,
As the sun's warmth kisses the earth,
And life begins its springtime weave.

Grant me balance in my mind and soul,
As I walk the path of wisdom and light.

Oh, powers of growth and renewal,
As nature bursts forth in bloom,
May my spirit find its fertile ground,
And dispel all shadows of gloom.

In this time of transition, I embrace,
The wisdom of opposites, the cosmic dance.

As daylight and darkness share this space,
Let balance reign in every place,
So mote it be, in harmony,
Blessed Equinox, a gift to thee.

BELTANE
Spring in Full Bloom
(May 1)

Beltane, celebrated around May 1st, is our second Grand Sabbat or Cross-Quarter holiday on the Wheel of the Year. Spring is now in full bloom and our senses are ignited! Spring embodies the fiery energy of passion, creativity, and fertility. As the Earth bursts into full glory and life awakens with unbridled enthusiasm we too celebrate our full selves coming back to life!

At Beltane, the Earth is adorned in vibrant hues of green and kissed by the sun's warming caress. Blossoms burst open, and the air is filled with the intoxicating scent of flowers and the hum of bees, birds and life itself. This is a season of sensuality, where the world is engaged in a passionate embrace, celebrating what it means to be alive.

Astrologically, Beltane aligns with the sun's passage through the zodiac sign of Taurus. Taurus is an earth sign, associated with sensuality, determination, and earthly pleasures. The energy of Taurus mirrors Beltane's themes of abundant growth and connection with the physical world. This is a time to get into your body and enjoy its powers!

Bonfires are a prominent feature of Beltane celebrations, and leaping over these fires (or dancing around them) is believed to purify and renew the spirit. The flames symbolize the energy of passion and transformation, and dancing around them is a way to embrace this fiery magic.

In Beltane's realm, the veil between the spiritual and physical worlds is thin, making it a time when the mystical and magical energies are potent. It's a season for casting love spells, harnessing the Earth's vitality for prosperity, and honoring the illusive and enigmatic spirits of the land.

Beltane Traditions

Beltane is a time for friends, families and communities to come together and celebrate the return of life on the spinning wheel. This is a time for lovers to frolic, for children to sing and dance and for everyone to celebrate the rising energy of the earth and their internal desires.

Maypole Dancing: Celebrate the divine union of masculine and feminine energies by weaving colorful ribbons together around the May pole. If you don't have an actual maypole just have fun dancing!

Bonfires: Light a bonfire for your community and gather around it to honor the sun's strength and power to renew and transform.

Flower Crowns: Honor the blooming beauty of spring flowers by making flower crowns and wearing them to your Beltane gatherings.

Handfasting Ceremonies: Beltane is a popular time for Pagan commitment ceremonies for couples. Hands are fasted together with ribbons while vows are exchanged.

Fertility Rituals: Ride the energy of Beltane by planting seeds or making offerings to the earth for a fertile growing season.

Greening of the Home: People decorate their homes with fresh greenery and flowers to bring the vibrant energy of spring indoors.

Jump the Fire

The word 'Beltane' in Celtic means "lucky fire" and this is the holiday to re-ignite your soul fire! Are you feeling distracted, overwhelmed or pulled in too many directions? Tap into the power of fire to release barriers, embrace your passions and bring action to your intentions!

Pagan communities typically come together at Beltane to sing and dance around a bonfire. Traditionally this was a celebration of the fertility of our bodies and the earth! Beltane is a time to embrace the power of your sexuality - to let your inner radiance shine and to glory in the radiance of others.

Another popular ritual is to jump the Beltane fire - embody the energy and take a leap forward in life towards your dreams!

Start by building a small fire in a safe location. If you can't build a fire outside then group some candles together inside (or even use electric candles for the safest option). Stand in a circle around your fire and bring your awareness to what you are calling in for your life and also what you are releasing.

Then, take turns running and jumping across the fire - as you leap over the fire let go of fear, regret, or indecision - let go of anything holding you back from the life you love living! Shout out loud your intentions if you'd like! Intentions are strengthened when shared in community and spoken to the Universe. Do this as many times as you are called to and cheer on your friends and family.

May the healing Beltane fire bring you transformation, energy and joy!

I Release...

The power of fire helps us to release and transform. There comes a moment when we have to let go of who we've been to become who we want to be. That moment is often a scary letting go of the past and a leap of faith into the future. Jumping the Beltane fire this year will help you take this leap of faith. But first, get clear on what needs to go to make room for the new!

The Wishing Tree

Beltane is a time of celebration but also a time to connect with nature spirits and practice rituals for health, prosperity, fertility and well-being. In Ireland and across the British Isles people still celebrate Beltane by hanging ribbons on small trees or shrubs, each of which represents their personal wishes for the coming season.

The Wishing Tree or Fae Tree is often found near sacred springs or wells. People in ancient times would take some clothing from a sick person and go and dip it into the sacred well and then tie it to a nearby tree to bring that person healing. The tradition has evolved to represent all wishes of well-being and abundance.

Create a Wishing Tree near you this Beltane!

Choose a tree or shrub close to you to be your Wishing Tree. Find some fabric - preferably made of natural fibers, and cut or rip it up into strips. Invite your friends and family to your wishing tree and have each person write their wishes and then tie them onto the tree. You can use different colors to invoke different wishes. Be gentle when tying your ribbons as to not hurt the tree.

Stand back and admire your tree. Feel all the blessings, prayers and positive intentions rooted there in front of you. Nurture your dreams as you nurture your tree.

Remember to also make an offering to the spirits of the land with food, sweets, egg shells, sea shells or other treasures. Offer gratitude for their help in making your wishes come true!

And so it is.

"Keep a little fire burning,
however small,
however hidden."

CORMAC MCCARTHY

Weaving Yin and Yang

Beltane is a time to celebrate the power of sexual energy! The earth is buzzing with life and the heartbeat of that life is attraction, energy and desire. We are dazzled by the brilliant and beautiful weaving of masculine and feminine energies entwined in their ancient, sacred dance. The archetype of the masculine and the feminine energies can help serve as a compass for how we can bring more balance into our lives. Although we see these energies in duality, they actually exists within all of us (and all living beings) regardless of our gender or sexuality. Bringing these forces into harmony empowers us to live our most purposeful and authentic lives.

Take some time today to think about how you are balancing your masculine and feminine energies. Do you tend to lean to one polarity or the other? Can you bring more heart to your head or more head to your heart? Can you strengthen your boundaries so your creativity can flow? Can you soften your thinking to make more space for feeling?

Bringing the masculine and feminine forces into harmony within you empowers you to live your most purposeful and authentic life. Embrace the light and the dark, the thinking and the feeling, the doing and the not doing, the giving and receiving! Somewhere amidst al of that circulating energy you will find your most authentic self, fully integrated, alive and magnetic!

Get ready to attract love, friendship, and abundance this Beltane!

Reflection

Do have enough masculine and feminine energy awakened in your life? How can you invite in more balance?

Sacred Sexuality

Sexual energy is potent, powerful, and sacred. At the root of our sexual energy is our desire. Desire drives life into action! Our sexual energy also carries the potential for opening doorways to other realms when we work with it in conscious and loving ways.

The sexual energy that we share with ourselves or with another, can help support the release of the old, and the invocation of the new.

Place your palms onto your lower belly with the tips of your index fingers and the tips of your thumbs touching. This creates a downward pointing triangle. This is a mudra that invokes the sacred, sexual energy of your second chakra, the Svadhisthana chakra who's mantra is "vam".

Drop into your breath and into your body, and with your hands in the downward facing triangle on your lower belly repeat the mantra "vam" (rhymes with "calm") 108x. Notice any thoughts or stories that arise in the mind, and just let them flow through. Let the vibration wash over and through you. Release any tension, trauma or stagnant energy and welcome in the new.

Your Svadhisthana chakra is also the center of your creativity, your pleasure and your deep imagination. Thoughts, ideas, projects and maybe even people are ready to be birthed by you!

Speak this mantra out loud:

"My body is a sacred vessel, My body is wise, I listen to and respect my body. My sexuality is sacred, My sexuality is wise. I am a conduit for goodness, beauty, acred connection and divine creativity."

AND IT IS SO

"There is no passion to be found playing small - in settling for a life that is less than the one you are capable of living."

NELSON MANDALA

Self-love Ritual

In our culture it is hard to be alone. We are bombarded with messages that show us our happiness is reliant on relationship with others. Often this leads to our search for the "other" who will make us feel whole. Unfortunately however, looking outside yourself only creates a bigger hole inside you.

Self-love is the highest love. If we don't love ourselves we can't love another. Isn't it interesting how we can sometimes be more understanding, patient and forgiving towards others than we can towards ourselves?

Take a few moments today to think about all the reasons you love yourself. All the things you are good at. All of your special talents and traits. Think about how you make yourself happy and how you take care of yourself.

How do you make yourself laugh? How do you take care of your body? How do you care for your soul? How do you protect your dreams?

Self-care isn't selfish - it's essential!

Offer gratitude for your body, the air you breathe, your beautiful mind and your capacity to love deeply. Fall in love with yourself today.

Remember that you are never alone, you are part of the tapestry of life - your thread shining, unique and an integral part of the whole! Fall in love with yourself and the world will fall in love with you.

And so it is!

Self-love Reflection

How do you take care of yourself? How could you take better care of yourself?

_____
_____
_____
_____
_____
_____
_____
_____
_____
_____
_____
_____
_____
_____
_____
_____
_____
_____
_____
_____
_____
_____
_____
_____

Beltane Blessing

With the flames of Beltane, let passion ignite,
As intentions blaze on this sacred night.
May your aspirations soar, unbound,
And your visions take shape, profound.

In the dance of the divine,
Find your rhythm and let it shine,
Release the old and embrace the new,
May the universe's magic flow through you.

And it is so!

SUMMER

SUMMER

The wheel of the year keeps turning! The quarter of the year from Beltane to Lammas, or from mid-May through mid-September in the Northern Hemisphere, is the season of summer. We ride the surging tide of solar energy when greens blanket the earth, flowers blossom everywhere in all different colors, shapes and sizes, and fruit is ripe and juicy for us to enjoy!

The surging tide of energy from spring to summer is a metaphor for personal growth and transformation. It's a reminder that even after periods of dormancy or challenges, we have the potential to burst forth with renewed energy, creativity, and passion. This shift mirrors the cycles of life, urging us to embrace change and harness the warmth and brightness of our own inner summers. As we move from the gentle awakening of spring to the exuberant energy of summer, we are reminded to cherish the beauty of growth and the vibrancy of life.

Summer season brings to life the elemental energy of fire. The fire energy of summer helps us manifest the intentions we planted earlier in the year through our effort and right action. Fire is what helps us turn food into energy and energy into our work in the world. Fire is the passion, determination and courage that drives us forward day after day and summer is the season to celebrate all that we have accomplished and the culmination of the cycle.

Absorb the Vitamin D into your skin, charge your third eye and celebrate the power, beauty, warmth and generosity of the Sun shining into you this summer! Enjoy the long days and longer sunsets. Take time to swim, walk, ride bikes, visit with friends and enjoy sweet fruit and ice cream cones!

Life is there for the taking. Live your best life with these summer rituals to help you shine your light on the world!

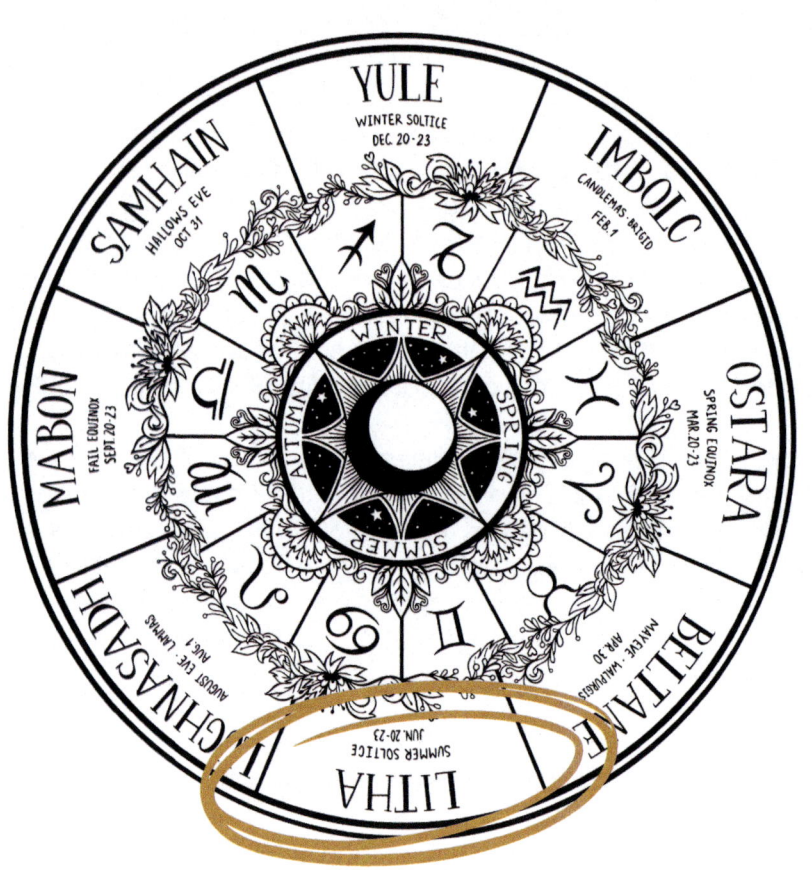

LITHA
Summer Solstice
(June 19 - 22)

At midsummer, when the Sun stands still, we celebrate the solar festival of Litha. Also known as the Summer Solstice, Litha occurs when the Sun moves into Cancer, generally between June 19-22 each year in the Northern Hemisphere. This is when the Earth's tilt towards the Sun is at its maximum, corresponding to the Sun's transit into Cancer, the sign of home, family, deep emotions, and sensitivity. The solstice portal continues for another three days as the sun seems to "stand still" in the sky before it starts back in the opposite direction.

There is a feeling of exuberance through all of nature with vibrant color, fragrance, song, dance, feasts and celebrations. The Sun sets late into the night and arises early in the morning, not leaving much time for rest. Instead, this is the time of year you may find you don't need as much sleep, you have a lot of energy and you are doing the things you love.

And although Litha is a celebration, it is a bittersweet moment, as the Sun has reached the height of its power and will soon begin to wane as the wheel continues to turn. For our ancestors this meant thinking ahead to the cold, dark days of winter and hoping for an abundant harvest to see them through.

Midsummer is a time to affirm your loves, savor the fullness of life, and fill up on all the good things. So, go out into the world - travel, explore, bimble - go the places where you feel most alive and savor the warm embrace of nature.

Your winter dreams and spring intentions are now coming to fruition. Be proud of how far you've come and how much you've grown. Take stock of your accomplishments and share in their glory with the people you love.

Open to being infused with sunlight through your entire being. Invite more occasions of generosity and non-judgment as you emulate the Sun, shining on everyone and everything. Invoke radiance in everything you do and let your light shine bright out into the world!

"Winter is copper,
autumn is bronze,
spring is silver,
and summer is gold."

MATSHONA DHLIWAYO

Litha Traditions

Litha, or Summer Solstice, marks the height of summer, the longest day of the year and the most light. In the far northern hemisphere the swings between darkness and light are intense - in Scotland the longest day is 18 hours leaving only 6 hours of darkness for sleep! This day is bittersweet - gratitude is given for the sun's abundance but also there is awareness that now the sun will start to fade as we enter fall - the time of year to harvest and release.

Bonfire: Light a bonfire or a small fire pit in your backyard or at a beach. Gather around with friends and family, sing songs, tell stories, and enjoy the warmth and light of the fire.

Sun Salutations: Practice yoga or perform sun salutations facing the rising or setting sun. It's a beautiful way to connect with nature and honor the sun's energy.

Outdoor Picnic: Plan a picnic with seasonal fruits. Blow your friends away with a beautiful fruit mandala!

Flower Crowns: Create flower crowns using fresh flowers and wear them as a symbol of the season's beauty and abundance.

Music and Dance: Organize a dance party with friends where you can dance under the stars and be merry! Make new friends.

Celebrate the summer solstice in a way that brings you joy!

Your Solstice Altar

Welcome and honor the glory and beauty of Litha's light with an altar! Maybe it's time to clean up and change over your current altar or maybe it's time to build a new one somewhere in your house our outside in nature.

Feel into the energetic imprint of Summer on your heart. Reflect on your unique experiences of this season over the years. What has summer meant to you throughout your life? Has it changed? How can you honor this time in an authentic way? Let your soul's vision come forward, illuminating and awakening midsummer magic in the form of your altar!

Create a south-facing altar space as the Summer Solstice is situated at the southern part of the Wheel of the Year. The South is also the direction of the element of fire - so dear to us in summer! Clear and cleanse your space by dusting, smudging or ringing bells.

Then, bring in items of gold, yellow and orange color along with summer flowers, fruits and vegetables. Find crystals that match the season like clear quartz or tiger eye, and collect depictions of any solar deities or spirits that you honor. Create an offering of flowers and sugar water for the fire spirits and their allies: bees, butterflies and pollinators. Invoke divine sweetness, ecstasy, and joy.

Connect to the nature spirits of your land and offer gratitude. And, as Hafiz advises, "Keep squeezing drops of the Sun."

Summertime

What does summer mean to you? What memories do you have? How are you making the most of this summer?

"The sun does not shine
for a few tress and flowers,
but for the wide world's joy."

HENRY WARD BEECHER

Solar Greetings

DAWN (OR ON RISING)

I arise today with the sun of hope and expectation. May the wisdom of my dreams guide my steps. I greet the new day as I go forth.

MIDDAY

I greet the fullness of the day with joy. May the strength and power of the sun help me engage with the work of my hands, so that blessings may be shed on all whom I meet.

TWILIGHT (OR AFTER WORK)

I come home on the wings of twilight, returning to the place of my true abiding. As the sun sinks in the West, may there be blessing upon my home and family as I return.

MIDNIGHT (OR ON GOING TO BED)

I lie down with gratitude for the gifts of today. I enter the darkness where wise dreams await me. Moonlight enfold my body, starlight bless my soul as I rest this night.

Lion's Gate Ritual

The Lion's Gate Portal is a powerful astrological and energetic event that occurs annually between late July and early August and is usually celebrated on August 8. It is believed to be a significant time for spiritual growth, awakening, and manifestation!

The portal gets its name from the alignment of the Earth, the star Sirius, and the Sun, creating a gateway of heightened cosmic energy. During this period of intensified energy, we earthlings can harness it by connecting to our Highest Self and focusing on our deepest desires for ourselves, our families and the world.

To make the most of the Lion's Gate Portal which is exact on August 8th but lasts a few days on either side, carve out sacred time for ritual. Find a quiet space where you can be alone. If you are inside light a candle, if you are outside, go somewhere that you can feel the warmth of the sun on your third eye.

Sit comfortably and take a few deep breaths. Feel your connection with the earth as you send energetic roots down from your core into the womb of Gaia. Connect with the energy of fire from your candle or the sun. Then, close your eyes and visualize that you are a big cat - a lion, or a tiger or whatever cat you most connect with. In your mind's eye, see and feel yourself perched on a rock overlooking the ancient savanna. Then, gently move and stretch your body like the big cats that still roam the earth.

Now, come to a comfortable seated position. Feel your spine lengthen and gently lift your chin. Feel into your inherent power and dignity. Feel the inherent power and dignity of the lion, of the tiger, of the king and queen of the desert. Let this power fill you up with golden light, encircling you above, below, within and without in a golden ball of light.

In this moment of radiance and power, dedicate yourself in thoughts, words and actions for your highest good and the highest good of all beings everywhere! Lion King, Lion Queen, Protector of the Desert - it is time for you to rise in your full power. The world needs you. And so it is!

Reflection

What is your highest purpose and calling in this lifetime?

_____
_____
_____
_____
_____
_____
_____
_____
_____
_____
_____
_____
_____
_____
_____
_____
_____
_____
_____
_____
_____
_____
_____

Litha Blessing

Radiant Sun, with golden rays so bright,
I call upon you in this sacred rite.
Oh, mighty Helios, Sun God divine,
Your warmth and light, upon us, shine.

Grant us strength and courage in this hour,
Fill our hearts with your radiant power.
Bless us with vitality, energy, and might,
As we honor you on this sacred night.

Oh, Sun God, source of life's sacred flame,
We honor you, we praise your name.
Accept our offerings, both heartfelt and true,
As we celebrate the Solstice, we honor you.

"May I have the courage today
To live the life that I would love,
To postpone my dream no longer
But do at last what I came here for
And waste my heart on fear no more."

JOHN O'DONOHUE

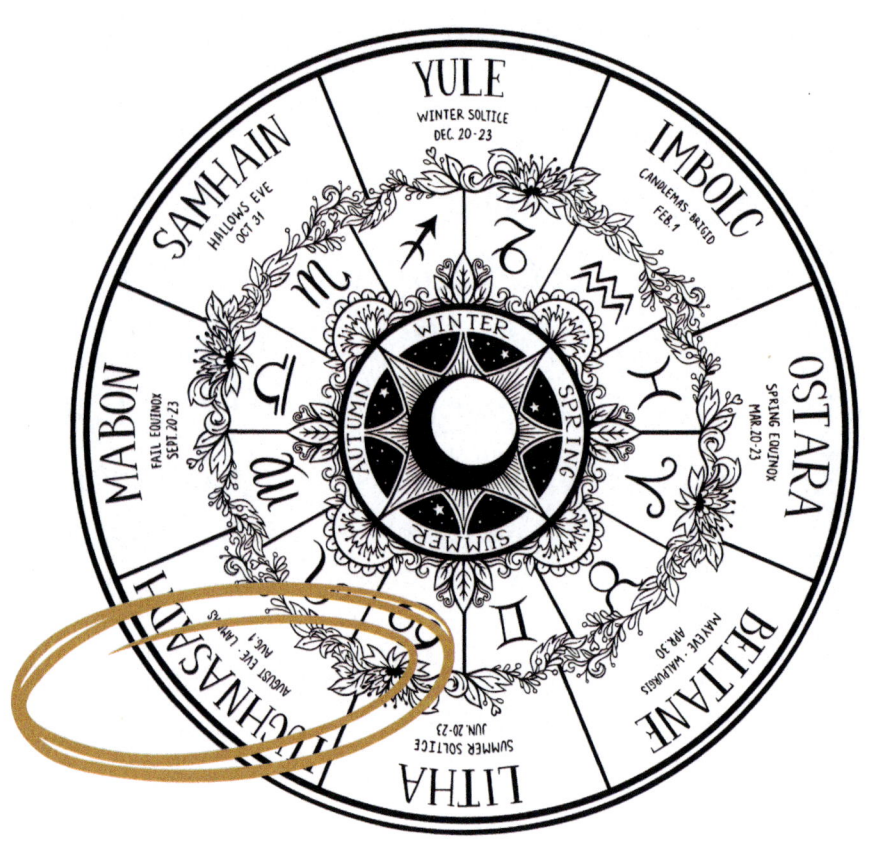

LAMMAS
The First Harvest
(August 1)

Lammas (also known as Lughnasadh) is a Grand Sabbat or Cross Quarter holiday that occurs midway between the Summer Solstice (Litha) and Fall Equinox (Mabon), usually celebrated on August 1. On Lammas we celebrate the culmination of the summer and the threshold into autumn, into the time of year when we slow down, reflect on our blessings and begin to harvest all we have sown throughout the year.

Solar Lammas with the Sun at 15 degrees of Leo encourages us to shine boldly and brightly. It is an energy of mastery and incredible skillfulness.

Lunar Lammas, on the day of the Aquarius Full Moon opposite the Sun in Leo reminds us to live in the paradigm where "ME" in all my bright glory is ultimately in service of "WE" – the collective, the land, and all that is. It is a balanced alignment highlighting the joy of Leo alongside the responsibility of Aquarius.

The personal empowerment of this season is in sharing your mastery with full hearted devotion to your craft. Play without fear of losing. Celebrate all the wins and the losses. Cheer each other on. Bless out loud everyone and everything. Show gratitude for all the gifts that come when hard work and dedication are combined with divine will and guidance.

Recognize the unique light in each person, envisioning and manifesting a world of thriving interdependence where everyone belongs. Shine bright and give thanks this Lammas Day!

Lammas Traditions

In the Celtic world, the hard work of the harvest season was balanced by a Lammas celebration that would extend for days. There would be games, races, music, dancing, and marriages,. These gatherings lifted up the greatness and goodness of the human spirit in relationship to other humans, animals, plants and the Earth.

Storytime: Share family stories! How far back can you go? Share stories of abundance, travel, adventure and sacrifice. What gifts and traits have your ancestors passed to you and what will you pass on to future generations?

Appreciate Music: Play music, listen to music and dance to music with your friends and family! Let go of your worries and get into your body. Release through music and dance like people have been doing for millenia!

Contracts: This is the time of year to review, update, clear or cancel relationships and business contracts. Take an objective look at what is working or not working for your finances.

Enjoy the Harvest: Bake bread, pick berries or enjoy the bounty at a local farmers market.

Host Friends: Host a dinner party to celebrate your friends and family and offer gratitude for your blessings.

Get Outside: Enjoy the changing colors of the season by getting outside and going for a hike. Check out new areas near you!

Spiritual Harvest

Activate the bright golden magic of abundance this Lammas with this simple ritual. Feel free to modify this ritual to make it your own. There is no wrong way to create ritual. Have faith in your own unique creative expression!

This ritual can be performed indoors or outside in a sacred place in nature. But, you will need space to walk! Begin by standing firmly on the earth, closing your eyes, and taking a few deep breaths. Feel your hands and your feet. Ground into the earth below you and open to the sky above you. Clarify your intention to align with the bright and shining energies of the season.

What energy is shining through you? Are you grateful? Are you proud of yourself? Are you hopeful? Focus on your deepest and truest feeling at this moment in time.

Then, starting in the east, walk in a clockwise circle, humming a sound that rises up from the earth, through your feet, legs, spine, and heart. This might be a song or mantra that you love or maybe it's a simple expression of your current feeling like "thank you" or "I love you" or "I am ready". Whatever it is, hum it out loud as you walk in a circle. As you move in this way, you are casting a circle of power. Within this circle you are expanding your intention – sending it out and into the wide world around you.

Pause at each of the cardinal directions and offer peace and additional blessings or acknowledgements:

Turn to the East: "May there be peace in the East."
Invite the element of air to expand your vision.

Turn to the South: "May there be peace in the South."
Invite the element of fire to activate your courage.

Turn to the West: "May there be peace in the West."
Invite the element of water to fill your life with abundance.

Turn to the North: "May there be peace in the North."
Invite the element of earth to help you always remember gratitude for the many blessings of your life and the Earth.

Turn your attention to the center of yourself and your circle: "May there be peace within and without."
Invite the element of spirit to connect you to all that is.

Kneeling down, place your right finger tips on the ground and your left hand on your heart. Breathe into your sacred connection to the Earth. Have faith and trust in yourself and the inherent goodness of the world. With your heart filled with gratitude, you will manifest even more abundance into your world!

And so it is.

Lammas Reflections

What have you sacrificed to be where you are now? Who has made sacrifices for you? What are you harvesting at this time?

Lammas Altar

Celebrate the transition from the fiery energy of summer into the watery energy of autumn by updating and spending time at your altar. Contemplate what you are harvesting this season and what you are releasing as you move into the dark half of the year. Let your altar be the sacred space you go to when you need peace and clarity.

- Add autumnal colors like dark green, golden yellow, orange, red, and bronze.
- Create a harvest doll out of straw. Use natural materials to decorate your doll.
- Add an ear of corn to your altar in honor of the Grain Mother.
- Decorate with local seasonal fruit and flowers.
- Adorn yourself and your altar with crystals for this time of year including citrine, tiger's eye, moonstone and peridot.
- Pull a tarot card to guide you through the season!

When your altar is ready, cleanse it with incense, light a candle and sit for a moment. Contemplate the gifts of the season. Write in your journal and reflect on all that has come to pass since you first set your intentions at Imbolc, celebrated them at Beltane and now you reap what you have sown at Lammas.

And so it is!

Lamma's Blessing

May the blessings of the harvest be upon you,
May Lugh's light guide your way,
May your heart be as full as the summer's bounty,
As the promise of the season gives you hope this day.

May the sun's rays shine brightest on your fields.
May your harvest be plentiful and your heart joyful.
May you find abundance in all aspects of your life,
As the Earth shows her grace upon you.

May you be strengthened and nourished in the year to come.
May all your work yield joy, success, and fulfillment.
May you reap the fruits of your efforts
As you enjoy great blessings and prosperity.

FALL

We now ride the falling tide from summer to fall. During the quarter of the year from Lammas to Samhain, (August 1 - November 1) we welcome the gentle release of nature. As the days grow shorter and the sun's intensity wanes, a shift in energy occurs, marking a period of reflection, transformation, and reaping what we have sown.

At Lammas, there is a subtle shift in the quality of light, a reminder that the Sun's power is gradually waning. We offer gratitude for the abundance of the earth and reap the rewards of our own efforts.

As we move from Lammas to Mabon, the autumnal equinox, the balance between day and night is briefly restored. This is a time of balance and harmony, symbolized by the sun's entry into the cardinal air sign of Libra. It's a reminder to evaluate our lives, release what no longer serves us, and seek equilibrium.

Samhain, marking the beginning of November, is the culmination of this energetic shift. Astrologically, it aligns with the sun's passage through the intense and transformative water sign of Scorpio. This is a time when the veil between the physical world and the spiritual realm is believed to be thinnest, making it ideal for honoring the dead and seeking guidance from ancestors.

As the days grow shorter and colder, we are encouraged to turn inward, embracing the mysteries of life and death. It's a time to release old patterns and fears, much like the trees releasing their leaves. The energy of Fall encourages us to dive deep into our own psyche, confront our shadows, and emerge transformed and renewed.

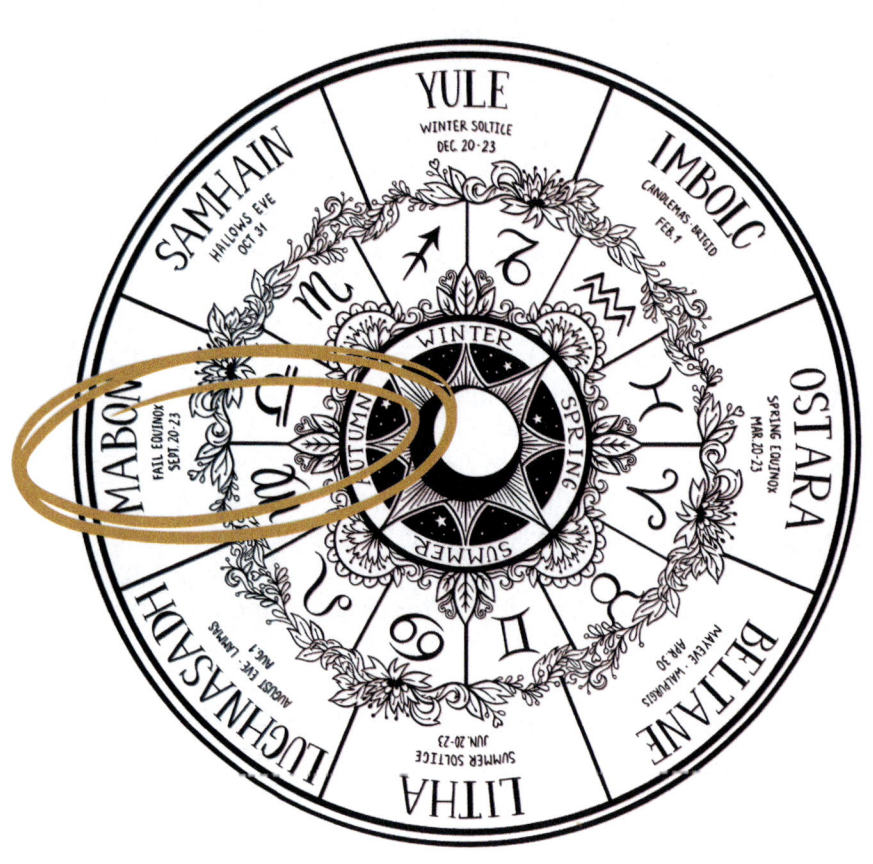

MABON
The Second Harvest
(September 21 - 23)

With a deep exhale, we welcome the seasonal energy of autumn. On the Wheel of the Year autumn is associated with the direction of the west and element of water. The element of water keeps us nourished, cleanses us, heals us and teaches us how to go with the flow and take the path of least resistance. Surrender to the deeper currents of your life this season and trust in your flow!

The Autumn Equinox, or Mabon, is a day of cosmic balance and the peak of Fall, marked by the moment when the Sun enters Libra, usually between September 21st to the 23rd. In pagan traditions, this day is celebrated as the Witches' Thanksgiving and the Second Harvest.

Honor this golden moment of Cosmic Balance when day and night are equal. Pause for a moment and feel into the balance: giving and receiving, harvesting and releasing, dark and light. The divine paradox of this season is recognizing that all that begins also ends and endings are beginnings in the cycle of life.

This is a time of gathering, harvesting and sharing in the way of reciprocal generosity. Make magic by creating cozy rituals of cooking, baking, enjoying time with friends, walking familiar paths and noticing the daily changes reflected in nature. Speak often of your gratitudes and blessings.

On Mabon, make a prayer to be in greater harmony with All That Is. Make this prayer, blessing or intention one that is large enough to embrace the polarities of life on Earth, one that can hold the dark and the light.

And in the words of mystic, Meister Ekhart, "If the only prayer you ever say in your entire life is thank you, it will be enough."

Mabon Traditions

We come to the point on the Wheel of the Year when we welcome in the dark half of the year. Mabon marks that threshold, briefly balancing light and dark before tipping towards the darkness. This is a time to close up loose ends, hunker down and get into a routine that supports you - mind, body and spirit. Here are some ideas to make Mabon special this year!

Nature Mandala: Go outside and create an offering to the spirits of your land by making a nature mandala.

Be in Service: Be in service to the Earth! How can you offer love and act on your love? Maybe pick up trash or volunteer at a local animal shelter.

Spirit Walk: The veil between the seen and unseen worlds is thinning. Go outside and walk with the spirits. Listen to the wind. Rest in a sacred grove or near a sacred well. Walk without a destination and see where you end up.

Harvest: Harvest your garden and use your own fruits and vegetables to make a cornucopia for your kitchen table.

Anoint Yourself: Find an essential oil or flower essence that you like and then mix it with a carrier oil and include a few drops of magically charged moon water. Use it to clear and ground your energy.

> We have so much before us
> and for this we are thankful.
> We have so many blessings,
> and for this we are thankful.

Bless This Day

Enacting a ritual simply means that you act with intention. Ritual is the time and space you set aside to join your internal heart desires with the external, material world. One way to live in reverence is to go through your day offering blessings to everything! Bless your feet touching the floor, your toothbrush that keeps your smile white, your fresh drinkable water, your energy-bringing coffee or tea, your co-workers, your sacred technology that keeps you connected, your magical car, and so on and so on!

When we look closely we have SO MUCH to be thankful for. Uplift your spirit and turn your thoughts towards possibility, unlimited potential, abundance, and deep nourishment for you and all beings everywhere!

Try weaving a short and simple prayer into your daily life. Say it out loud when you wake up, when you are eating, when you enter a building or home and when you go to bed at night. See how you feel and what happens in your life when you keep this positive intention at the forefront of your mind. Write it below and let the magic flow!

"Gratitude is the prayer.
Take stock of the blessings received,
and succumb to tranquility."

SYBIL DANA REYNOLDS

Earth Mandala

A nature mandala is a circular design of gathered leaves, sticks, stones, seeds, nuts, flowers, or any natural wonder. Making a mandala is a fun and creative way to connect with nature and the nature spirits of your land. Explore the materials that are available to you. Available to all without having to purchase, kill or make them!

The first step is to go outside and find a place you would like to make an offering to the Earth and the spirits of the land where you live. Kneel for a moment to ground and connect with the energy of the land and receive the consent of any elemental spirits that inhabit that space.

Then, look around you and gather materials. There are usually many symbols of fall at your feet! Start building your mandala, piece by piece, being present with the textures, scents, colors, and feelings of the materials. If you are making this with another person, don't try to control it, just let it flow. Starting in the center and working your way out, think of something you are grateful for with each placement. Connect with all the ways the Earth, and the land where you live, supports you.

Then, sit down near your mandala and place your right hand to the Earth and your left hand to your heart. Inhale energy from the Earth into your heart and exhale your hopes, dreams and thanks into the Earth. Stay in this gesture of divine connection for as long as feels good. When you are done, leave your mandala for other earth spirits to enjoy.

"Nature's peace will flow into you as sunshine flows into trees. The winds will blow their freshness into you, and the storms their energy, while cares will drop away from you like the leaves in Autumn."

JOHN MUIR

Equinox Water Ritual

With water as the element associated with Mabon, perform a simple water ritual. Water is a beautiful element to work with in ritual because it soaks up energy and then can infuse that magical energy in you from the inside or out!

To start, find a clear glass bowl and fill it with fresh, clean spring water. Leave this bowl of water charging on a windowsill where it can soak up the energy of both the Sun and the Moon in the day/night of the Equinox.

Then, when you are ready for your ritual, take your bowl of water and create your sacred space. Maybe call in a circle, or make a physical circle around you. Sit in the center and contemplate water's elemental wisdom while holding your bowl on your lap.

First, surrender to the Vast Unknown. Then, ask for the energy of the water to help you:

- Clear weariness, worries, hurts and burdens.
- Hold your heart open with space for all your feelings.
- Flow with the ever-changing tides and rhythms.
- Let the ocean's salt heal your wounds.
- Remember your truth and essence as a fluid being, capable of change.

Feel your water charge with all of these beautiful intentions! Then, use this Equinox Essence water to anoint your body and nourish yourself from the inside by drinking it. Welcome in the healing and wholeness!

Reflections

How do you give and receive? Do you give more than you take? Do you take more than you give? Can you find balance in reciprocity?

Mabon Blessings

May all be welcome at the feast table.
May you celebrate the harmonious balance
of all that is, embracing the polarities of life on Earth.

May you drink deeply of the Cup that overflows
with love – never thirsting, never hungering.
May you be in this time betwixt and between
with peace and grace.

May the days and nights ahead bring you
deep peace and sweet rest.
May you be blessed, protected and nourished
in all the years to come.

Blessed Be this Mabon!

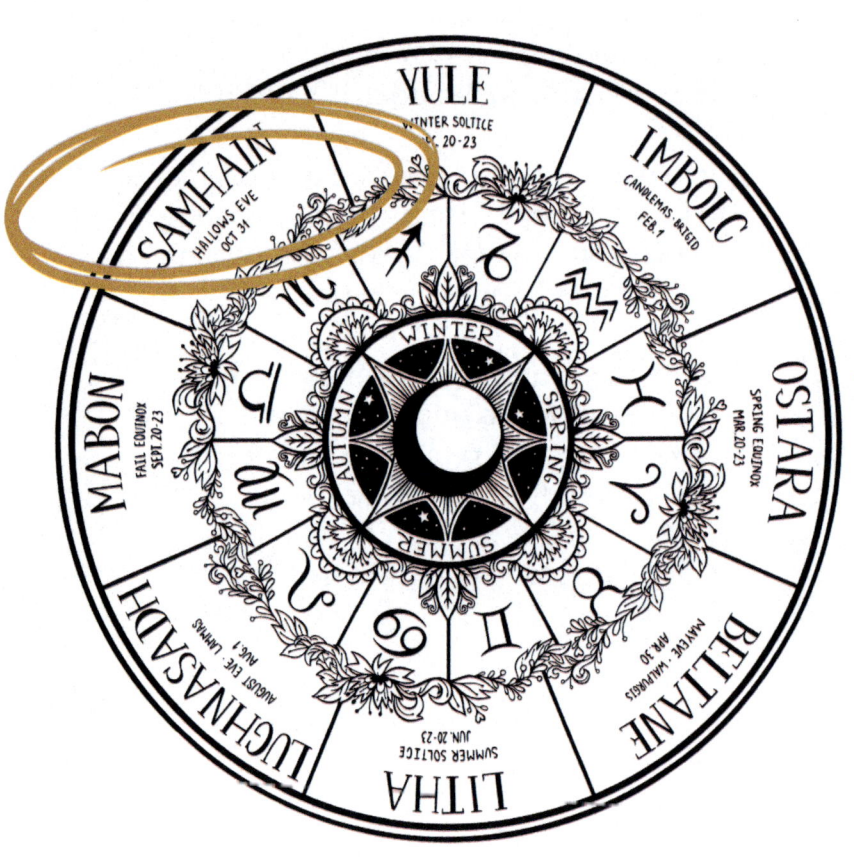

SAMHAIN
Witches' New Year
(October 31)

Samhain Blessings! Samhain (pronounced "Sow-wen") ushers us into the most potent and mysterious time of year when anything is possible! On Samhain night, bring out all your witchy ways, light the candles, stir the cauldron and feel the magic deep in your bones.

Samhain originates from the Gaelic, "samh fuin", meaning "summer's end." It's a festival of the final harvest, and a celebration of all that have passed before us. After the Samhain festivals, any remaining fruit, berries and nuts were left as an offering for the birds and fae.

As the veil thins, we remember those who have passed over to the Otherside. We build altars in our hearts and homes for our beloved dead. We leave them offerings. We listen for their messages in our dreams, meditations and journal musings. We also shift the energy with costumes, decorations, and treats - through play, we open to other ways of being and interacting with the seen and unseen.

Samhain is celebrated on the same day as Halloween. Samhain is connected to Scorpio season in astrology, a deep, intense, and seductive energy. It is one of the most magical and mysterious of signs, interested in what is not seen and not said with "normal" senses.

This energy supports massive transformation and shadow work to end karmic patterns and start again in an entirely new way. Scorpio and Samhain season invites you to reckon with that which you've cast into shadow and darkness (both fears and desires), and ultimately reclaim your authentic power.

This most magical of seasons, when the veil is thin and even the most cynical scientist hears whispers from the Otherside, we celebrate the great Mystery of life itself and turn within to our strongest sense of faith as we say goodbye to what was with hope in our hearts that all will be reborn.

"I'm so glad I live in a world where there are Octobers."

L.M. MONTGOMERY

Samhain Traditions

Samhain, or Halloween, is the time of year when everyone is open to getting a bit weird, a bit witchy and ready to dabble in the dark arts! How can you not when we are inundated with ghosts, goblins, witches and warlocks everywhere we look? The fact is that Halloween has become big business in the US, with an estimated $12B spent on Halloween candy, decorations and costumes in 2023 alone.

But, there are more ancient, more powerful and less consumptive ways to celebrate the true energy of the season. Get inspired by our recommendations below!

Samhain Altar: Each Sabbat you have the opportunity to honor the season at your altar and Samhain is no exception. This is the season to get out your black candles, your crows, your divination mirrors, your crystals, your moonwater and of course your cauldron!

Honor your Ancestors: Honor those that came before you by bringing out and dusting off their photos. Put them on your altar or other places in your home. Research them, tell their stories and remember them!

Simmer Pot: Infuse your home with good smells and good vibes by making a simmer pot. Simply simmer a pot of apple cider with cinnamon sticks and oranges on your stove to infuse your home!

Decorate your Threshold: The threshold of your home is the portal between your internal and external worlds. Sweep it clean, decorate it and let the good spirits of your ancestors know they are welcome!

Practice Divination: When the veil is thin we can connect to the Spirit would more easily and clearly. Inquire about your future using a pendulum or tarot cards. Be open to the messages that come through!

Beloved Ancestors

As you move through this Samhain season, speak the names of your beloved ancestors. Place their photos on your altar. Light candles for them. Give them flowers. Cook their favorite foods and set them a place at your table. Your beloved ancestors live on through memories of their lives. Help keep them alive and well this Samhain by honoring those that came before you and teaching the young people in your life the importance of this tradition.

Remember, too, the ancestors of the land you currently call home. Find out who they were and how they lived. Leave them an offering of gratitude for sharing their land with you.

It's important to acknowledge when talking about our ancestors that not all of them were necessarily "good". We may have ancestors that did things in the world that hurt or oppressed or abused others. While this may be true, we still owe them gratitude for our lives. And, we can continue the journey of evolution through our own healing and awakening process.

In this lifetime we can reconcile the wounds - given and received, while reclaiming our own healing wisdom, magic and power. What you heal in this lifetime and timeline, heals all who came before and all who come after. Honor their lives through honoring your own.

> Let it begin with each step we take,
> And let it begin with each change we make,
> And let it begin with each chain we break,
> And let it begin every time we wake!
> -Starhawk

The Dumb Supper

Those who are remembered are not lost! The Dumb Supper is a Samhain ritual for ancestral remembrance and honoring.

Invite your ancestor(s) to a feast. Create a centerpiece altar with candles, flowers and photographs. Set a place for each of your living guests and beloved dead.

Light a candle and set an intention to connect with ancestors along your Blood and Soul lineages, and through them, to connect with your own personal magic and reason for being here.

Wait in silence for them to arrive at your table and in your consciousness. Ask questions as if in dialogue with ancestors sitting with you at the table. Open to the Otherside and let their answers flow through you in a stream of consciousness way.

What would Dad have said? What would Grandpa have wanted to eat? What would Aunty Nell have said about the dinner? Tell their stories, laugh, write down their favorite sayings. Most of all, take the time to remember each of them for the unique energy they brought into the world - including you!

At the conclusion of the ceremony, place their food outside as an offering.

With a thankful heart, dine and share Samhain's blessings! What is remembered, lives!

Re-member us,
you who are living,
Restore us, re-new us
Speak for our silence
Continue our work
Bless the breath of life
Sing the hidden patterns
Weave the web of peace.

JUDITH ANDERSON

RIP Ritual

One of Samhain's lessons is to let die what is dying so you can let live what is living.

The Rest in Peace ritual is designed to be performed on the Dark Moon before the Scorpio New Moon - a most sacred night of the year suffused with the power to transform via death and rebirth.

It takes so much courage to be here in full presence; embracing the entire cycle of life, facing fears, completing karma, ending old programs and habitual limitations, and truly experiencing freedom.

For this ritual you will need 3 bay leaves and an apple. Then, ask yourself:

What is ready to die?
What karma is complete?

Keeping it short, write it on your bay leaves. When you are done writing, repeat 3 times: "As my word, so mote it be."

Then, go outside and find a place where you can dig a hole in the dirt. Bury the leaves with your messages along with the apple. The apple is an offering to the spirits of the land and to the Great Spirit of Gaia to help you let go of what no longer serves.

Gently tap the earth and whisper "Rest in Peace" - and it is done.

Know Thy Shadow

As Fall turns to Winter we bring our awareness inside for reflection and contemplation. This is the time of year when we are open to the darkness, aware of the inevitability of death, and curious about the deeper currents of our lives. This is a time ripe for practicing Shadow Work.

Shadow Work is a term coined by psychiatrist and psychotherapist Carl Jung. It refers to looking at the parts of you that you don't see and that your ego doesn't identify with and therefore you have no awareness of. These may also be traits in yourself that you don't like or accept. Shadow Work challenges you to look at all the parts of yourself in order to take control of your life and not let shadow emotions and fears run the show.

If you find yourself running to stand still, going through the motions, or consistently dealing with negative situations, thoughts and emotions, it might be time for you to try Shadow Work. Shadow Work can be difficult because contrary to a lot of spiritual self-help, which focuses on love and light, it digs deep into the darkness, the pain and the fear - with the goal of illuminating the unconscious and rooting out the shadows that hold you back. That said, Shadow Work is not for the faint of heart. If you have experienced trauma it may be better to work through your past with a mental health professional.

One concept in shadow work that can help you gain the vision and clarity to make necessary changes in your life is the concept of accepting radical responsibility. Often, we blame others for how we are feeling or the circumstances of our lives. That blame can be masking your shadow.

Can you take radical responsibility for every aspect of your life? If things are not how you want them can you recognize your own part in the situation? By recognizing your own behaviors, you can choose to react differently and exercise greater empowerment.

Try this today! If there is a negative situation in your life, take time to think about how you can take radical responsibility over it.

Are there ways that your actions are feeding into the situation? Are you looking for approval, avoiding the hard truth, or lacking trust in yourself? Dig deep into the recesses of your unconscious mind and you might find a shadow lurking there that is no longer wanted. The good news is, when this shadow pops up again you will recognize it and instead of going on auto-pilot, you will call your own bluff and get on with solving the problem, for your Highest Self and all beings everywhere!

Journaling can be a safe and therapeutic way to work with your shadow. Try answering the questions on the following pages to work with your shadow. Be sure to take care of yourself when practicing these exercises - create a safe and nurturing space and give yourself time to process when revelations or memories come up.

May these questions help open you to your highest truth!

Shadow Journal

What did I need but not get during my childhood? How is that affecting me now?

Do I put my own needs first? Where do my physical, emotional and spiritual needs fall in relation to everyone else's?

Do I trust myself? Do I consistently make decisions that align to my own highest good? If I don't, why not?

When things are hard what do I do? What is it about the situation that I find the hardest? What is it I am most scared will happen?

What do I keep hidden from people? What am I good at, or love or believe in that I don't let others see?

What is my biggest dream for my life? If I had no fear, what would I do? How would my life be different?

Book of Shadows

A Book of Shadows is a journal dedicated to your magical workings and companion to your rituals. In it, you gather spells, invocations, herb lore, recipes, inspiring words, healing, dream messages, synchronicities and divination practices. It is the place where you remember and store all the magical experiences of your life so you can look back and remember you are Divine Magic.

Create your Book of Shadows today!

Begin with a blank journal. Decorate the cover with a collage of images that resonate with your personal brand of magic.

Do you identify as a witch? What type of witch are you? Solitary, coven, hereditary, folk, priestess, crystal, cosmic, activist, kitchen, green, ceremonial, hearth and home, elemental, sex...or a delightful and unique mixture of all of the above?

Or, if not a witch are you a mermaid, a unicorn, a sloth, a hedgehog, pegasus, a nymph, a centaur, a dragon, a great whale, a fairy, an elf, an alien or some other magical creature?

Ground yourself and then cast a circle of blessing and protection (elaborate or simple, calling in the elemental powers and invoking peace in the east, south, west and north). Then get to decorating! Let this book be an expression of your soul magic! When you are finished, charge your book with the power of the elements - swirl it with smoke or incense, dab it with oil, sprinkle it with water, and dash it with a pinch of salt or crumble of dirt.

May this book help you remember your magic and kindle your creativity for years to come!

Samhain Blessings

May you look with clear vision beyond the veil,
Seeing what is, was and will be with truth.
May you know that death is not the end,
But a transition and a transformation.

May you be blessed by the ancestors,
Remembering them with thankfulness,
Their legacy alive in your heart,
Rebirthed through sacred light.

Blessed be this Samhain night.

Spin the Wheel

We hope this journey through the seasons of magic has deepened your connection to Nature, Spirit and Self.

The seasons, just like our lives, are in a constant state of flow, an unstoppable force through space and time. Embrace the power to change, to direct your will, to grow, to learn, to celebrate and to release. This is the wisdom inherent in the germinating seed, the blooming flower and the falling leaves. It is in these moments of transformation and transition that the most potent magic can be found.

May you continue to live your life in reverence and ritual for many cycles of seasons and for generations to come.

And so it is. And so it shall be!

Blessed Be

And the circle is open but never broken.

SAGED

Printed in Great Britain
by Amazon